T0198906

An Illustrated Explanation of Automatic Disconnection of Supply.

Well co-ordinated Automatic Disconnection of Supply is the key element of efficient Electrical Power Distribution & Fire Alarm Systems!

D.W. Cockburn

illustrationexplains.com

AuthorHouse™ UK
1663 Liberty Drive
Bloomington, IN 47403 USA
www.authorhouse.co.uk
UK TFN: 0800 0148641 (Toll Free inside the UK)
UK Local: 02036 956322 (+44 20 3695 6322 from outside the UK)

Because of the dynamic nature of the Internet, any web addresses or links contained in this book may have changed
since publication and may no longer be valid. The views expressed in this work are solely those of the author and do not
necessarily reflect the views of the publisher, and the publisher hereby disclaims any responsibility for them.

Any people depicted in stock imagery provided by Getty Images are models,
and such images are being used for illustrative purposes only.
Certain stock imagery © Getty Images.

This book is printed on acid-free paper.

ISBN: 978-1-4490-5537-0 (sc)

Print information available on the last page.

Published by AuthorHouse 11/27/2020

authorHOUSE®

Introduction:

Electrical circuits must be protected not only against overload, but also against short circuit. Protection against both may be afforded by a device known as an Over-current Protective Device, which can be in the form of a Fuse, a Circuit Breaker or a Residual Current Circuit Breaker with Over-current Protection.

The over-current protective device therefore protects the cabling of the installation, it does this by having similar characteristics to the cable that it is intended to protect, only being slightly weaker under all circumstances.

Therefore whether for example the problem is a huge overload due to a sudden short circuit, or a long drawn out overload possibly caused by a faulty device or appliance; the over-current protective device shall automatically disconnect the supply before any permanent damage can be done to the cabling it is protecting.

For these reasons Automatic Disconnection of Supply is provided by an over-current protective device and is used:

To protect Electrical 'systems' from problems that may occur within an individual 'circuit', whilst allowing the remainder of the 'system' to continue functioning normally.

To protect Electrical 'circuits' from problems that may occur within an individual 'device or appliance', this time allowing the remainder of the 'circuit' to continue to function normally.

The amalgamation of the Electrical Installation Standards between Britain & Europe, offer a variety of different options with regard to wiring methods relevant to Automatic Disconnection of Supply, whilst limiting options with regard to component part design.

The aim of this book is to explain with the help of simplified illustrations: efficient automatic disconnection arrangements and circuit configurations, for various types of Electrical Power Distribution and Fire Alarm systems.

Diversity:

Making good use of 'diversity' will have a positive impact on the 'efficiency' of an electrical installation. The objectives are; to supply appliances using the minimum size of cable, in order to keep <u>installation costs to a minimum</u> and, to automatically disconnect the supply before the cabling can be overloaded, in order to keep <u>running/maintenance costs to a minimum</u>.

When applying 'diversity' we can simply work on the principle that more than one appliance can be supplied via the same cabling at different times, but we can also consider safely exceeding a circuits' stated maximum 'current carrying capacity' for limited periods of time without fear of damaging its' cabling."

For example 2 x 3Kw appliances will draw 6000watts of power, dividing this by a nominal supply voltage of 240volts we find that we will need to supply a circuit capable of carrying 25amps.

Therefore a 25amp 'ring' final circuit will supply 2 x 3Kw appliances simultaneously.

But because of the nature of over-current protective devices we know that our 25amp device will happily cope with a load of 37.5amps, or 3 x 3Kw appliances working simultaneously, for up to an hour before automatically disconnecting the supply.

As 99.9% of the time, at least one of our simultaneously operating appliances' thermostats will certainly come up to temperature within an hour; under normal working conditions 3 x 3Kw appliances will be very unlikely to overload a 25amp over-current protective device.

However when one of our three appliances becomes old or faulty and begins to draw too much current; the result will be that when all three of our appliances' thermostats call simultaneously, more than 37.5amps will need to be supplied and the over-current protective device will automatically disconnect the circuit, within less than an hour.

For example, when a washing machines' and 'faulty' tumble driers' thermostats are calling simultaneously and then we plug in a kettle, the kettle won't have time to boil before the trip operates.

This should result in the prompt repair or replacement of the faulty tumble drier!

Therefore, the closer that the circuits' total 'load current demand' is matched to its' 'current carrying capacity', the more efficient installation costs and clients' running and maintenance costs can be!

POWER DISTRIBUTION

Single outlets – 'Spur' final circuits

The following drawings represent the simplest '1gang socket outlet' or 'double pole switch', supplied by a 'spur' final circuit configuration.

The current carrying capacities represented are of the two most commonly used types of cable, when installed using the two most commonly used installation methods.

Twin and Earth cable (T&E) – clipped direct (Ref. Method 'C')

Singles in Conduit/Trunking (SinC) – on a wall (Ref. Method 'B')

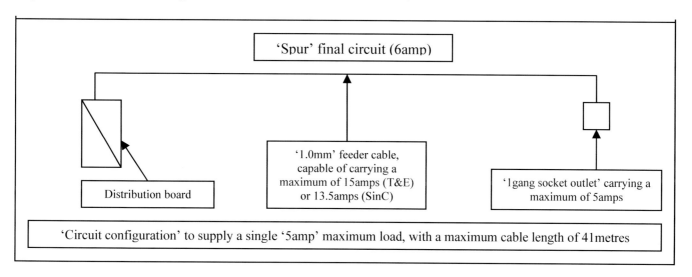

In order to provide 'over-current' protection to a circuits' cabling, options are governed by the maximum 'current carrying capacity' of the cable, which must be <u>greater</u> than the 'minimum breaking current' (Prospective fault current @ 10 000 secs.) of the over-current protective device that is intended to be used.

The maximum size of over-current protective device, with a 'minimum breaking current' of less than, the maximum 'current carrying capacity' of 1.0mm Singles (13.5amps) and/or T&E (15amps):

A 'BS 1361' 5amp cartridge fuse (in the plug top, if 13amp socket outlets are used)

Type B, C or D 'BS EN 60898' 6amp circuit breaker (approx. 8.6amps)

Type B, C or D 'BS EN 61009' 6amp RCBO (approx. 8.6amps)

The maximum length of the circuit will be restricted by 'voltage drop' over distance; for 1.0mm Singles or T&E:

Maximum load current x Voltage drop (per ampere per metre)

5amps x 0.044v = 0.22.

Maximum volt drop 230v x 4% =9.2v.

9.2v / 0.22 = 41metres.

Note: If 'un-fused' 5amp plugs are to be used, they must be used in conjunction with at least 1.0mm (max. 9.5amp) flex!

In order to reduce the size of the flex, a 13amp plug top containing a 3 amp fuse will need to be used.

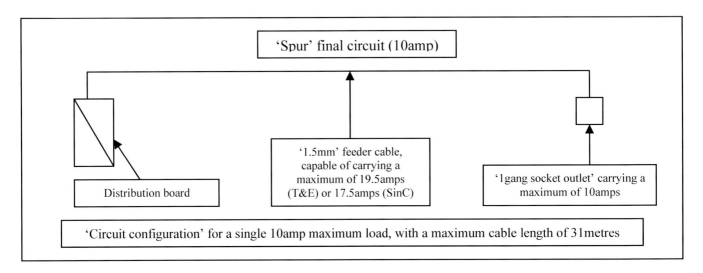

The maximum size of over-current protective device, with a 'minimum breaking current' of less than the maximum 'current carrying capacity' of 1.5mm Singles (17.5amps) and/or T&E (19.5amps):

A 'BS 1361' 10amp cartridge fuse (plug top).

Type B, C or D 'BS EN 60898' 10amp circuit breaker (approx. 15.33amps)

Type B, C or D 'BS EN 61009' 10amp RCBO (approx. 15.33amps)

The maximum circuit length restricted by volt drop for 1.5mm Singles or T&E:

Maximum load current x Voltage drop (per ampere per metre)

10amps x 0.029v = 0.29.

Maximum volt drop 230v x 4% = 9.2v.

9.2v / 0.29 = 31metres.

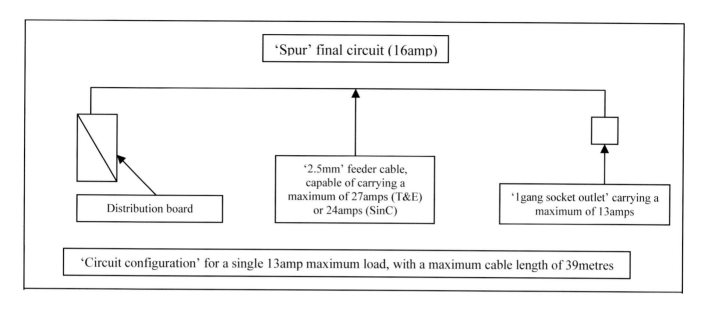

The maximum size of over-current device, with a 'minimum breaking current' of less than the maximum 'current carrying capacity' of 2.5mm Singles (24amps*) and/or T&E (27amps):

A 'BS 1361' 13amp cartridge fuse (plug top).

Type B, C or D 'BS EN 60898' 16amp circuit breaker (approx. 23.33amps)

Type B, C or D 'BS EN 61009' 16amp RCBO (approx. 23.33amps)

*Note: Where 'correction factors' apply, while the over-current protective device remains the same, cable size may well need to be increased in order to compensate!

The maximum circuit length restricted by volt drop for 2.5mm Singles or T&E:

Maximum load current x Voltage drop (per ampere per metre)

13amps x 0.018v = 0.234.

Maximum volt drop x 4% = 9.2v.

9.2v / 0.234 = 39metres.

Correction Factors:

The 'current carrying capacity' of cable must be multiplied by 'correction factors' associated with Grouping and/or Ambient Temperature and/or Thermal Insulation, where they apply.

Extremely low 'correction factor' values that will greatly reduce the effective current carrying capacity of cables, associated with for example; large groups of circuits contained within a common trunking, or cable(s) being surrounded* by thermal insulation, or extreme ambient temperatures during the summer months can theoretically cause the need to increase the size of any supply cabling.

Within these pages, the circuit configurations where 'correction factors' are most likely to have such a negative influence, have been *__Noted.__*

Please note: When Twin and Earth cable is 'clipped directly' to ceiling joists etc. one side of the cable will always be flat against the timber, therefore neatly clipped cables need never be literally 'surrounded by thermal insulation'.

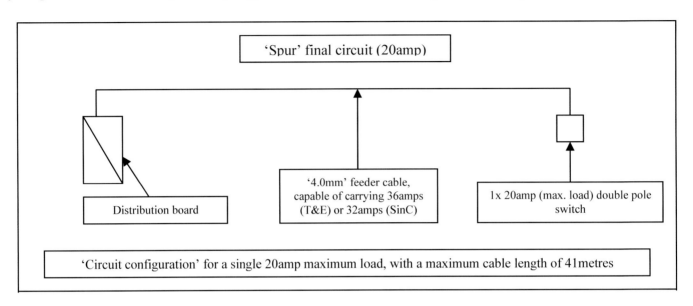

The maximum size of over current protective device, with a 'minimum breaking current' of less than the maximum 'current carrying capacity' of 4.0mm Singles (32amps*) and/or T&E (36amps):

Type B, C or D 'BS EN 60898' 20amp circuit breakers (approx. 29amps)

Type B, C or D 'BS EN 61009' 20amp RCBO (approx. 29amps)

Note: Where 'correction factors' apply, while the over-current protective device remains the same, cable size may well need to increase in order to compensate!

The maximum circuit length restricted by volt drop for 4.0mm Singles or T&E:

Maximum load current x Voltage drop (per ampere per metre)

20amps x 0.011v = 0.22.

Maximum volt drop x 4% = 9.2v.

9.2v / 0.22 = 41metres.

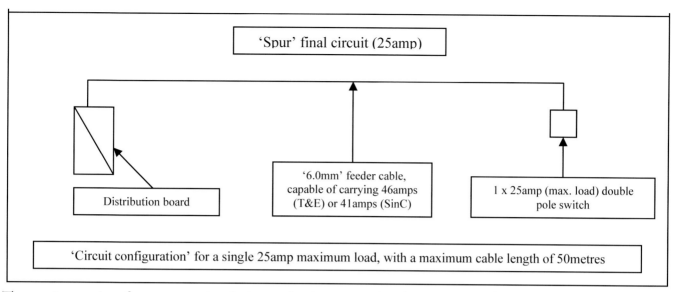

The maximum size of over-protective device, with a 'minimum breaking current' of less than the 'current carrying capacity' of 6.0mm Singles (41amps) and/or T&E (46amps):

Type B, C or D 'BS EN 60898' 25amp circuit breakers (approx. 36.66amps)

Type B, C or D 'BS EN 61009' 25amp RCBO (approx. 36.66amps)

The maximum circuit length restricted by volt drop for 6.0mm Singles or T&E:

Maximum load current x Voltage drop (per ampere per metre)

25amps x 0.0073v = 0.1825.

Maximum volt drop x 4% = 9.2v.

9.2v / 0.1825 = 50metres.

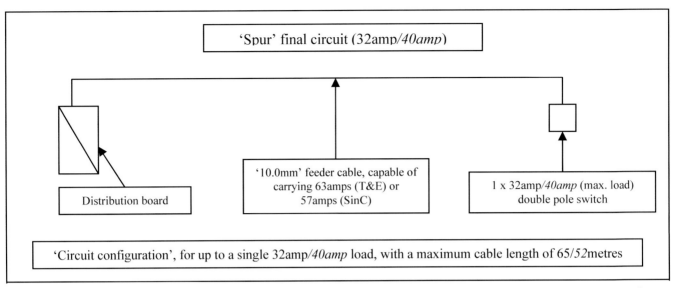

The maximum size of over-current protective device, with a 'minimum breaking current' of less than the maximum 'current carrying capacity' of 10.0mm Singles (57amps) and or T&E (63amps*):

Type B, C or D 'BS EN 60898' 32amp circuit breakers (approx. 46amps)

Type B, C or D 'BS EN 61009' 32amp RCBO (approx. 46amps)

Or if 'correction factors' do not reduce current carrying capacity of the cable to less than 57.5amps; 10.0mm T&E (63amps):

Type B, C or D 'BS EN 60898' 40amp circuit breakers (approx. 57.5amps)

Type B, C or D 'BS EN 61009' 40amp RCBO (approx. 57.5amps)

The maximum circuit length restricted by volt drop for 10.0mm Singles and T&E:

Maximum load current x Voltage drop (per ampere per metre)

32amps (Singles or T&E) x 0.0044v = 0.1408

Maximum voltage drop x 4% = 9.2v.

9.2v / 0.1408 = 65metres.

40amps (T&E) x 0.0044v = 0.176

9.2v / 0.176 = 52metres.

'Radial' systems

Please note: 'Spur' final circuits, supplied via the same Distribution Board may be collectively described as:

A 'radial' system - *a "Network of single feeders supplied from a single source", or a "Distribution system in which single supplies are given as 'spurs' from a main distributor"*

Radial – *"Having spokes or lines that 'radiate' from a central point"*

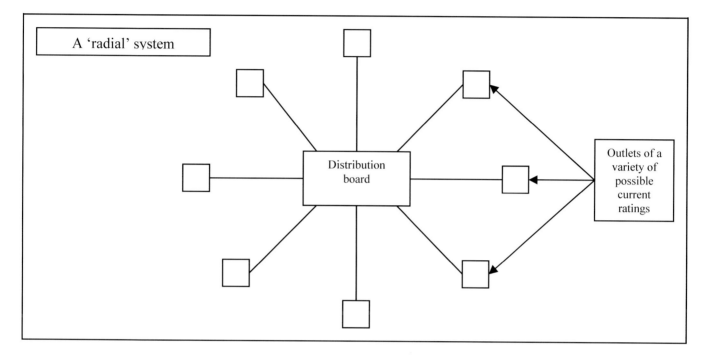

Multiple socket outlets – (Sequentially wired) 'final' circuits

Where there is a need to supply multiple appliances; it is necessary to add their respective load current demands together, making sure they do not exceed the maximum 'current carrying capacity' of the circuit.

The following drawings represent multiple 'socket outlets' supplied by 'final' circuit configurations.

The current carrying capacity of a 'final' circuit and therefore the size of over-current protective device for a 'final' circuit is identical to a 'spur' final circuit arrangement, given the same size and type of cable.

The length of a 'final' circuit will, as with the 'spur' final circuit be restricted by 'voltage drop' over distance.

Note: *For ease of continuity testing and maintenance, it is important to try to keep all of the 'terminations' easily accessible.*

Generally these objectives are achieved by arranging 'final' circuit socket outlets one after another, in a sequence.

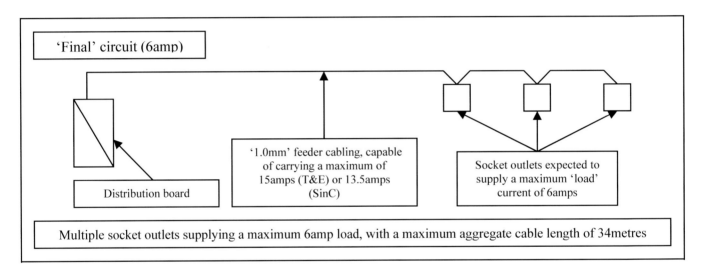

'Final' circuit (6amp)

Distribution board

'1.0mm' feeder cabling, capable of carrying a maximum of 15amps (T&E) or 13.5amps (SinC)

Socket outlets expected to supply a maximum 'load' current of 6amps

Multiple socket outlets supplying a maximum 6amp load, with a maximum aggregate cable length of 34metres

The maximum size of over-current protective device with a 'minimum breaking current' of less than the maximum 'current carrying capacity' of 1.0mm Singles (13.5amps) and/or T&E (15amps):

A 'BS 1361' 5amp cartridge fuse (in the plug top, if 13amp socket outlets are used)

Type B, C or D 'BS EN 60898' 6amp circuit breakers (approx. 8.6amps)

Type B, C or D 'BS EN 61009' RCBO (approx. 8.6amps)

The maximum circuit length restricted by volt drop for 1.0mm Singles or T&E:

Maximum load current x Voltage drop (per ampere per metre)

6amps x 0.044v = 0.264.

Maximum volt drop 230v x 4% = 9.2v.

9.2v / 0.264 = 34metres.

Therefore, if the maximum load current cannot exceed 6amps **(also see 'Diversity')**, it is possible to use up to 34metres of 1.0mm Singles or T&E to supply any number of outlets.

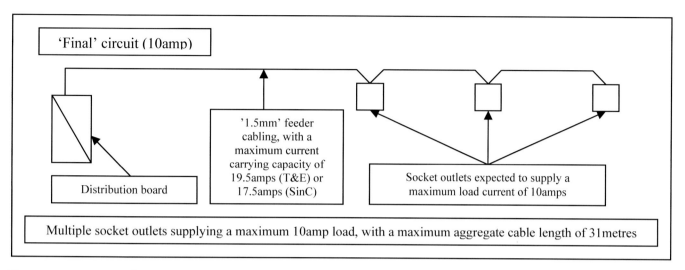

The maximum size of over-current protective device with a 'minimum breaking current' of less than the maximum 'current carrying capacity' of 1.5mm Singles (17.5amps) and/or T&E (19.5amps):

A 'BS 1361' 10amp cartridge fuse (plug top)

Type B, C or D 'BS EN 60898' 10amp circuit breakers (approx. 15.33amps)

Type B, C or D 'BS EN 61009' 10amp RCBO (approx. 15.33amps)

The maximum circuit length restricted by volt drop for 1.5mm Singles or T&E:

Maximum load current x Voltage drop (per ampere per metre)

10amps x 0.029v = 0.29

Maximum volt drop 230v x 4% = 9.2v

9.2v/0.29 = 31metres

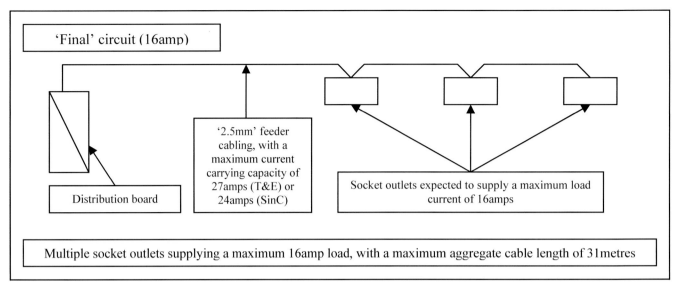

The maximum size of over-current protective device with a 'minimum breaking current' of less than the maximum' current carrying capacity' of 2.5mm Singles (24amps*) and/or T&E (27amps):

A 'BS 1361' 13amp cartridge fuse (plug top)

Type B, C or D 'BS EN 60898' 16amp circuit breakers (approx. 23.33amps)

Type B, C or D 'BS EN 61009' 16amp RCBO (approx. 23.33amps)

*Note: Where 'correction factors' apply, while the over-current protective device remains the same, cable size may well need to be increased in order to compensate!

The maximum circuit length restricted by volt drop for 2.5mm Singles or T&E:

Maximum load current x Volt drop (per ampere per metre)

16amps x 0.018v = 0.288

Maximum volt drop x 4% = 9.2v

9.2v/0.288 = 31metres.

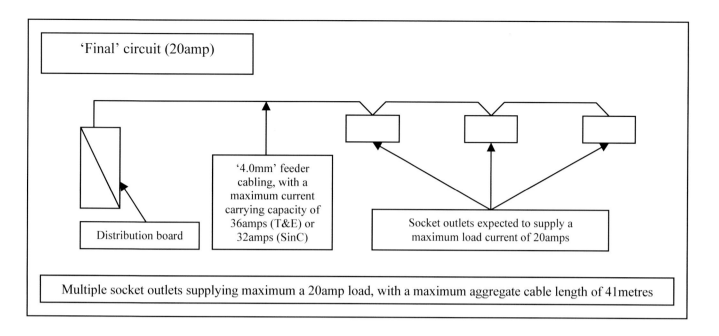

The maximum size of over-current protective device with a 'minimum breaking current' of less than the maximum 'current carrying capacity' of 4.0mm Singles (*32amps) and/or T&E (36amps):

A 'BS 1361' 13amp cartridge fuse (plug top)

Type B, C or D 'BS EN 60898' 20amp circuit breakers (approx. 29amps)

Type B, C or D 'BS EN 61009' 20amp RCBO (approx. 29amps)

*Note: Where 'correction factors' apply, while the over-current protective device remains the same, cable size may well need to be increased in order to compensate!

The maximum circuit length restricted by voltage drop for 4.0mm Singles or T&E:

Maximum load current x Voltage drop (per ampere per metre)

20amps x 0.011v = 0.22

Maximum volt drop x 4% = 9.2v

9.2v/0.22 = 41metres.

Multiple socket outlets – 'ring' final circuits

In order to increase a circuits' current carrying capacity without having to increase the cable size, it is possible to configure cabling into the shape of a 'ring'.

The following drawings represent multiple 'socket outlets' supplied by 'ring' final circuit configurations.

The current carrying capacity of a 'ring' final circuit is greater by a factor of 1.67 than that of a 'final' circuit or a 'spur' final circuit, given the same size and type of cable.

The length of a 'ring' final circuit will, as with the 'final' circuit and the 'spur' final circuit, be restricted by 'volt drop' over distance.

However it is generally accepted that a 'ring' final circuit is measured by the area it can cover, rather than by the length of its' cabling.

Note: *Now that a 'Residual circuit device' must be used to protect all circuits containing 'socket outlets' supplying portable equipment, a 'residual circuit device tester' may be used to confirm correct 'polarity' throughout a 'ring final' circuit!*

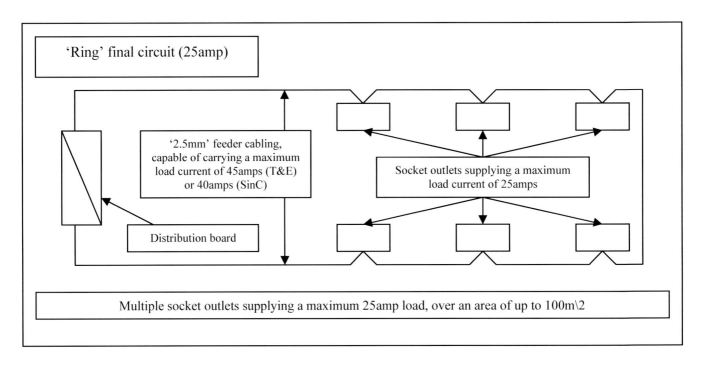

'Ring' final circuit (25amp)

'2.5mm' feeder cabling, capable of carrying a maximum load current of 45amps (T&E) or 40amps (SinC)

Distribution board

Socket outlets supplying a maximum load current of 25amps

Multiple socket outlets supplying a maximum 25amp load, over an area of up to 100m\2

The maximum size of over-current protective device, with a 'minimum breaking current' of less than the maximum 'current carrying capacity' of 2.5mm Singles (approx. 40amps) and/or T&E (approx. 45amps) when configured into a 'ring' final circuit:

A 'BS 1361' 13amp cartridge fuse (plug top)

Type B, C or D 'BS EN 60898' 25amp circuit breaker (approx. 36.66amps)

Type B, C or D 'BS EN 61009' 25amp RCBO (approx. 36.66amps)

The maximum area that can be covered by a 'ring' final circuit is generally accepted as being 100m\2.

A 'ring' final circuit may incorporate any number of socket outlets, as long as the maximum load current will not exceed the maximum current rating (25amps) of the circuit under normal running conditions. **(see 'Diversity').**

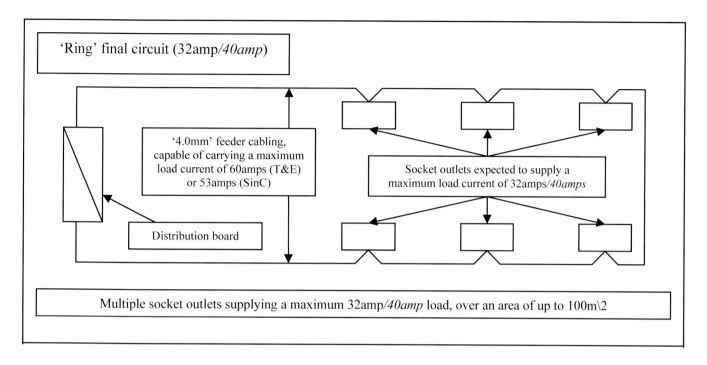

The maximum size of over-current protective device, with a 'minimum breaking current' of less then the maximum 'current carrying capacity' of 4.0mm Singles (approx. 53amps) and/or T&E (approx. 60amps*) when configured into a 'ring' final circuit:

A 'BS 1361' 13amp cartridge fuse (plug top)

Type B, C or D 'BS EN 60898' 32amp circuit breakers (approx. 46amps)

Type B, C or D 'BS EN 61009' 32amp RCBO (approx. 46amps)

Or if a 'correction factor' does <u>not</u> reduce current carrying capacity of the cabling too less than 57.5amps; 4.0mm T&E (approx. 60amps) when configured into a 'ring' final circuit:

Type B, C or D 'BS EN 60898' 40amp circuit breakers (approx. 57.5amps)

Type B, C or D 'BS EN 61009' 40amp RCBO (approx. 57.5amps)

The maximum area that can be covered by a 'ring' final circuit is generally accepted as being 100m\2.

A 'ring' final circuit may incorporate any number of socket outlets, as long as the maximum load current will not exceed the maximum current rating (32amps/*40amps*) of the circuit under normal running conditions. **(see 'Diversity').**

Spurring from a 'Ring' final circuit

*One extra '2gang, 13amp socket outlet' may be 'spurred' directly from any/all of the outlets on a 2.5mm <u>Twin and Earth</u> 'ring' final circuit.

If any more than two outlets are required, then they must be supplied from the 'load-side' of a 'fused connection unit' (spur box), which is supplied on its' 'feed-side' as a part of the 'ring' final circuit.

One extra '1gang, 13amp socket outlet' may be 'spurred' directly from any/all of the outlets on a 2.5mm 'ring' final circuit wired using <u>Singles in conduit/trunking</u>.

If any more than one outlet is required, then they must be supplied from the 'load-side' of a 'fused connection unit' (spur box), which is supplied on its' 'feed-side' as a part of the 'ring' final circuit.

The reason for the above is that a '2 x 13amp socket outlets' can supply a maximum load of 26amps, but unfortunately '2.5mm Singles' configured as a 'spur' can only carry a maximum load of 24amps!

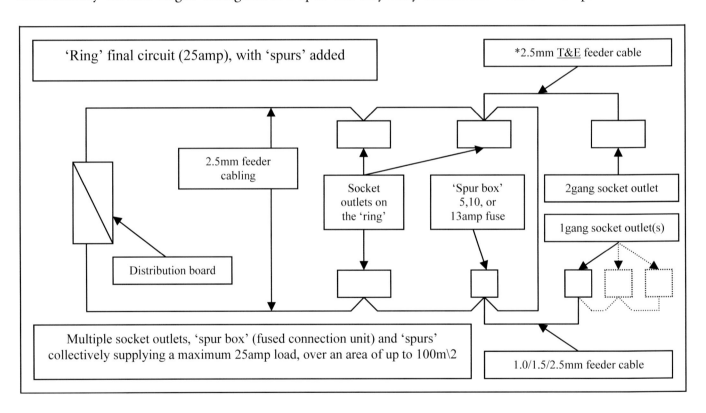

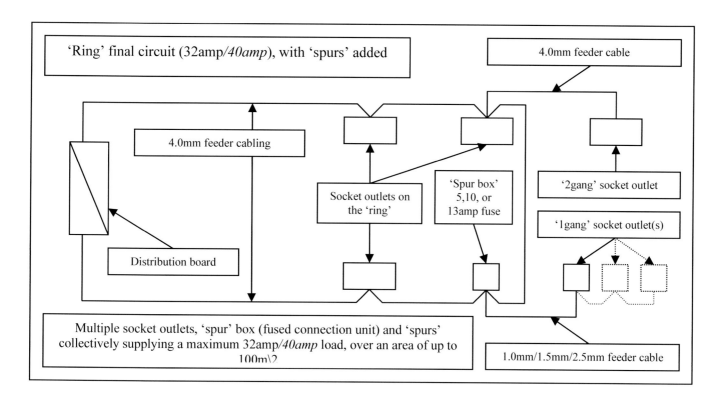

The diagram contains the following labels:

'Ring' final circuit (32amp/*40amp*), with 'spurs' added

4.0mm feeder cable

4.0mm feeder cabling

Socket outlets on the 'ring'

'Spur box' 5,10, or 13amp fuse

'2gang' socket outlet

'1gang' socket outlet(s)

Distribution board

Multiple socket outlets, 'spur' box (fused connection unit) and 'spurs' collectively supplying a maximum 32amp/*40amp* load, over an area of up to 100m\2

1.0mm/1.5mm/2.5mm feeder cable

'Radial' & 'Tree' final circuits

There are at least two other possible 'circuit configurations' that are worth considering; unfortunately they both share the common problem that they both incorporate inaccessible terminations within junction boxes!

The 'radial final circuit' if it is to cover as wide an area as it is intended to do, is reliant upon a 'central point'.

This 'central point' can only be some sort of a junction box, which must be positioned where the 'radial feeder' meets the 'stub end feeders'.

The 'tree final circuit' is reliant upon the use of a number of junction boxes, which must be positioned wherever a 'branch feeder' meets the 'trunk feeder'.

Both of these circuit configurations can certainly cover huge areas with regard to voltage drop, their current carrying capacities' will be the same as 'spur' or a *sequentially* wired 'final' circuit, given the same size and type of cabling.

It is the problems associated with the inaccessibility of the terminations at the 'junction boxes' that has led them to be generally shunned, especially by *local councils!*

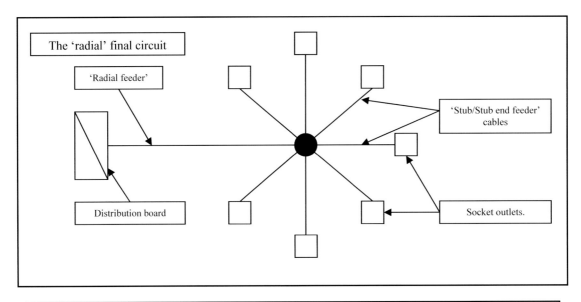

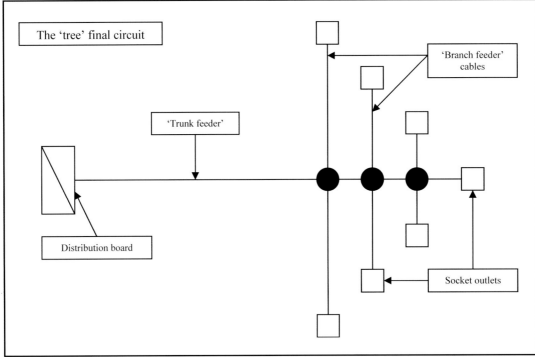

The maximum size of over-current protective device, with a 'minimum breaking current' of less than the maximum 'current carrying capacity' of a 'radial' final circuit or a 'tree' final circuit will be dependant upon cable size:

1.0mm Singles or T&E – 'BS EN' 6amp circuit breakers or RCBO (approx. 8.6amps)

1.5mm Singles or T&E – 'BS EN' 10amp circuit breakers or RCBO (approx. 15.33amps) etc

The maximum length of a radial final circuits' combined 'radial' feeder and 'stub end' feeder cables are restricted by volt drop over distance:

1.0mm Singles or T&E – 41metres

1.5mm Singles or T&E – 31metres etc

The maximum length of a tree final circuits' combined 'trunk' feeder and/or 'branch' feeder cables are restricted by volt drop over distance:

1.0mm Singles or T&E – 41 metres

1.5mm Singles or T&E – 31 metres etc

FIRE ALARM SYSTEMS

'Automatic disconnection of supply' can be used to prolong the operational ability of the essential components of a fire alarm system. Isolating fire alarm devices and/or their feeder cabling, if and when they become damaged whilst being exposed to the extreme temperatures of a fire, allows the rest of the system to remain operational.

This is achieved in exactly the same way as when 'automatic disconnection of supply' is used to isolate a faulty appliance from an electrical circuit, or to isolate a faulty electrical circuit from an electrical system.

The 'Radial Fire Alarm Sounder System' represented below, incorporates over-current/short circuit protection for each of its' essential devices individually within the CIE (control and indicating equipment).

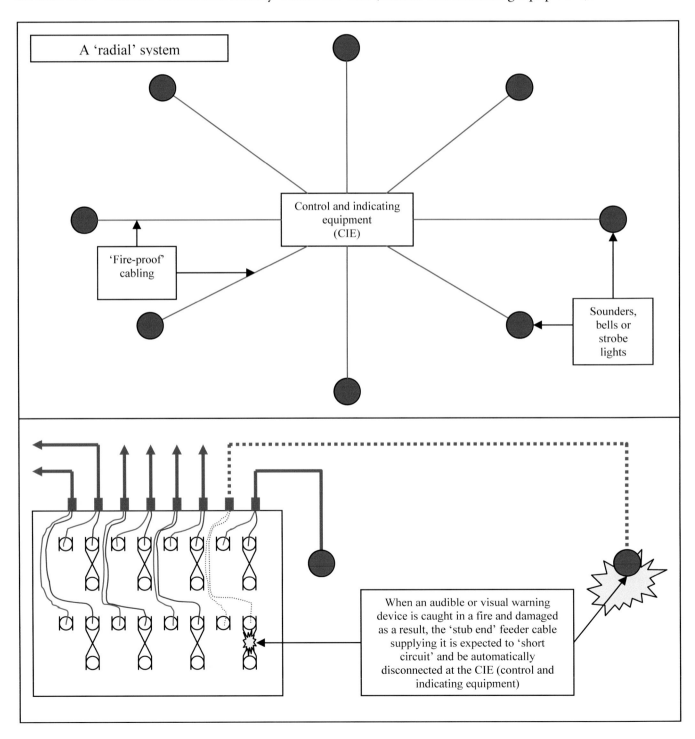

A 'radial' system

Control and indicating equipment (CIE)

'Fire-proof' cabling

Sounders, bells or strobe lights

When an audible or visual warning device is caught in a fire and damaged as a result, the 'stub end' feeder cable supplying it is expected to 'short circuit' and be automatically disconnected at the CIE (control and indicating equipment)

The 'Two Zone Fire Alarm Bell System' represented below, incorporates over-current protection for its' cabling within the CIE (control and indicating equipment).

Uniquely, short circuit/fire protection is supplied for each individual Bell; by the wafer thin flexes that connect the 'mineral insulated' feeder cabling terminated on the base of the Bell, to the electromagnet inside the dome of the Bell.

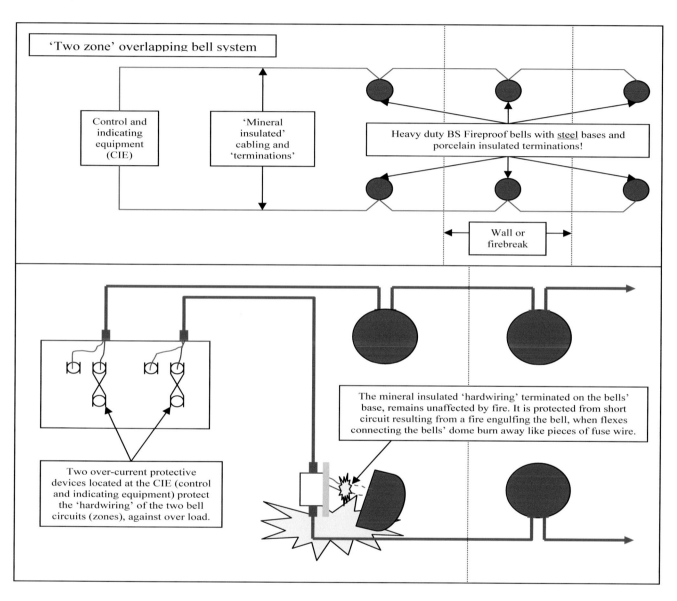

'Two zone' overlapping bell system

Control and indicating equipment (CIE)

'Mineral insulated' cabling and 'terminations'

Heavy duty BS Fireproof bells with steel bases and porcelain insulated terminations!

Wall or firebreak

The mineral insulated 'hardwiring' terminated on the bells' base, remains unaffected by fire. It is protected from short circuit resulting from a fire engulfing the bell, when flexes connecting the bells' dome burn away like pieces of fuse wire.

Two over-current protective devices located at the CIE (control and indicating equipment) protect the 'hardwiring' of the two bell circuits (zones), against over load.

The 'Loop Fire Alarm System' represented below, incorporates over-current/short circuit protection for each of its' essential devices, both within each of the essential devices themselves and within the CIE (control and indicating equipment).

Any device that causes a short circuit in the looped feeder cabling due to being engulfed in a fire; will cause <u>two</u> over-current/short circuit protective devices located within the two essential devices closest to it in each direction on the 'loop' (or one essential device and the CIE), to automatically disconnect the affected section of the 'loop'.

This process is referred to as 'short circuit isolation'.

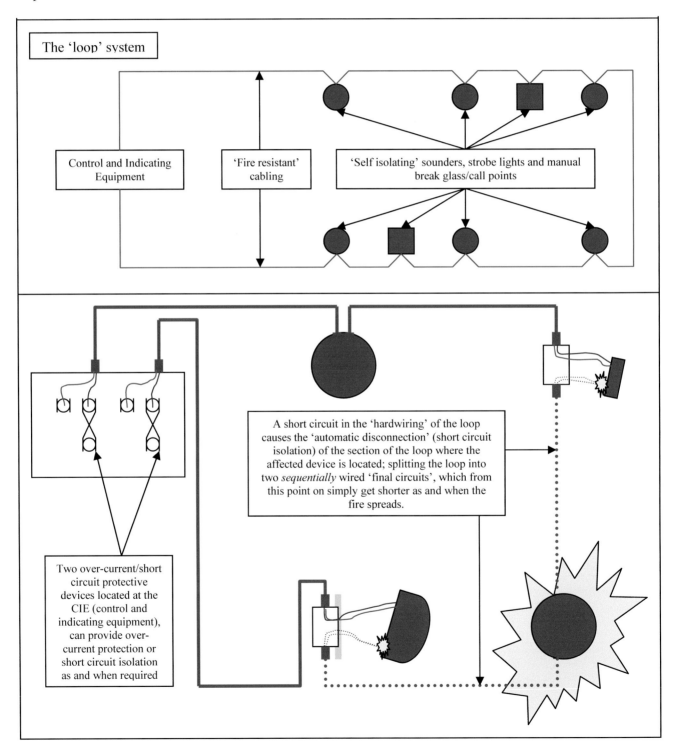

The 'loop' system

Control and Indicating Equipment

'Fire resistant' cabling

'Self isolating' sounders, strobe lights and manual break glass/call points

A short circuit in the 'hardwiring' of the loop causes the 'automatic disconnection' (short circuit isolation) of the section of the loop where the affected device is located; splitting the loop into two *sequentially* wired 'final circuits', which from this point on simply get shorter as and when the fire spreads.

Two over-current/short circuit protective devices located at the CIE (control and indicating equipment), can provide over-current protection or short circuit isolation as and when required

In conclusion:

Overloading an Electrical Circuit will over-heat the cabling that makes up that circuit!

When a cable is over-heated it will stretch and for a cable to stretch its' cross sectional area must be reduced. A reduction in cross sectional area will increase a cables' resistance to the flow of current.

Therefore once a cable has been overloaded it will be less able to carry its' original load, whilst actually adding to the resistance of the overall load through its' own reduced CSA.

Therefore a repeat of the original loading will need to draw more current in order to function as before, overloading the already weakened cabling even more than the first time and wasting huge amounts of energy in the process!

This spiral will then continue, until such time as the cables' insulation begins to melt away and arcing is allowed to occur!

Fire Alarm System, Audible and Visual Warning Devices are permanently transmitting a message!

If a person notices an audible or visual warning device during a fire and it isn't operating, the message being transmitted is that they appear to have reached a safe area away from the fire.

If an audible or visual warning device isn't operating because an entire zone or large part of a loop has failed during a fire, that fire is in reality likely to be very close by!

High volumes of human traffic or carelessly placed air conditioning equipment will accelerate the movement and quantity of airborne dust particles, likely to cause the failure of optical detectors!

Batteries will from time to time be: faulty/corroded/worn-out/stolen.

Automatic and battery powered activation devices are therefore undoubtedly prone to failure, mainly due to circumstances beyond the control of the system installer.

A Manual Call Point or Break Glass is therefore, an essential means of activating the fire alarm system!

If you were to smash a break glass and it failed to activate the Fire Alarm System, what would you do?

About the Author

David Cockburn is an Electrician who was given a start in the industry by his Father.

Nearly a decade and a half of practical experience preceded a highly successful college education, followed by a promising individual career in Electrical Installation.

Latterly David has spent his time educating himself in the field of British and European Electrical and Fire Alarm Installation Safety Standards.

Printed in the United States
By Bookmasters